Ian Kerr

testament
tales

by
Mary Stobo
illustrations by Iain Campbell

Parish Education Publications

First published in Great Britain
in 2002
by Parish Education Publications
21 Young Street
Edinburgh
EH2 4HU

ISBN 1904325025

Illustrations by Iain Campbell

Layout by Heather Macpherson

Printed by Datacolor Imaging

Contents

Introduction

The Bible is full of the voices of the folk whose stories have been told down through the generations. I've tried to hear these voices as they might have been heard as they told their tales to their friends and to people who might not know the background to their stories. Many of the tales therefore contain not just the personal experience but also glimpses of the tradition or of the countryside around or the context from which the situations arose. Such glimpses may help us to understand more of what was important to the people in the stories and so make them more meaningful for us.

The stories do not all follow the same format. This is because they have been used in different ways over the years. Most started life as simply told stories as part of a Sunday service, often as part of an 'all-ages' occasion. Then they were adapted for other uses such as informal adult study groups or small-group worship. You will find that some have a longer reflection, others have suggestions for music or activities depending on how they have been used. All have a prayer and some questions that you might like to consider. All are suitable for using for private reflection or as discussion starters in groups. From the variety included, I hope you will be able to see ways of adapting each of them to suit your own purposes. There is no right or wrong way!

Ideas for using the tales

- On your own as a start to thinking things through for yourself. You might like to record the thoughts that the questions provoke in a journal as you go along.
- The shorter ones could be told as a children's address – they love a well told story even without visual aids. Of course you could enlist the help of an artist in the congregation to draw the characters on a flip chart as you tell the story! Although you don't need to have the story off by heart you will need to be very familiar with it so that you have plenty of eye contact with your listeners of whatever age.
- As part of a Sunday service, as the set theme or to expand on the same passage in the Bible given as a reading. They can be used very effectively as the first part of an address, followed by a suitable hymn or song or other piece of music then a short, more 'grown-up' sermon which brings out the point you want to make. The questions can often help for this.
- A study group (perhaps the worship or education planning group) could work on a story beforehand and find a way of presenting their response to the larger congregation or help to identify the concerns that people would like to see covered in preaching or teaching.

• For a discussion starter for a study group. Don't feel you always have to use all of the questions. If you have a limited amount of time just do what you feel appropriate. Most of the discussions would need at least 30-45 minutes or longer but it does depend on the size of the group to some extent; more people equals longer time to hear what they each want to say.

Working with a group

It is helpful if you can use a variety of techniques. If you rely on people contributing as they wish, those with more confidence often dominate the discussion leaving others feeling left out, especially in a large group.

If you have had little experience in leading groups here are some well tried techniques you might find helpful:

Buzz

People talk in twos or threes to those sitting beside them so giving an opportunity for the quiet ones who would not speak up in a large group to have their say. The leader then takes feedback, usually writing up comments made on a flip-chart or whiteboard. Try to ensure that everyone is allowed to contribute something even if it is just to nod their head in agreement to what another buzz-group member has said. It's usually good to get one comment from each group then move on to the next until no new comments are left.

Silent wall (or Graffiti wall)

Put large sheet(s) of paper up where people can get to them easily. Have each sheet clearly headed with the question. Invite them to write up their comments in answer to the question(s) using thick pens to make them easy to read from a distance. Alternatively give out post-it type notes and ask for comments to go on those before putting them up. This is good if people are shy about having their contributions identified or if you want to sort comments into headings later.

Brainstorm

Ideas or comments are written up on a flip-chart without comment. No discussion should be encouraged unless it is just to make clear what the person meant. This is a good way of quickly collecting a response from a large group to identify what is important to them.

Plenary

Everyone has a chance to contribute (often as – or after – comments are collected from smaller groups). The leader may record on a flip-chart what has been said or it may just be a chance to talk about things together. Even with a smallish group it usually takes longer than you plan for and it can be very time - consuming in a large group where people are keen to contribute or are argumentative!

the blind man's tale

Mark 10:46-52; Luke 19:35-45

There were lots of people on that dry, dusty road. I heard the crack of a whip, the clink of harness and clatter of hooves as the rich folk drove by. The rhythmic clip of ridden horses muffled the scuff of sandals as the poor trudged along, some leading donkeys that brayed in annoyance in the heat. It was a steady stream of people, some on business, some with their minds and hearts set on worship. All going to Jerusalem.

The city was the place of pilgrimage for Jews who worshipped in the Temple there. It was also the seat of the Roman government in the area. There was a lot of civil service traffic on the road because Herod had built his magnificent palace in Jericho, away from the heat of the city on the hill. You'll have heard of Jericho (remember Joshua and the ram's horn?). It's been a favourite with rulers for centuries. Beautiful, so they told me. An oasis down in the valley with a much kinder climate where trees offer shade from the glaring sun and scent the air with resin. A lovely, cool green place. But that did mean that soldiers and messengers commuted regularly between the two places.

I'll never forget that day. It began much like any other. From my place at the side of the road I could feel the sun on my body. I could feel the grit sting my face as it was stirred up by the passers by and blown in the wind. I could hear the sounds of the people, even snatches of conversation and the Palm singing of the pilgrims. That never ceased to amaze me. How could they find the strength to sing as they walked up the long steep hills that led to the Holy City? I could smell the animals and the people through the dust that got up my nose but I could not see any of this cavalcade, for I was blind.

Suddenly there was a change in the sound. I sensed a crowd of people coming towards me. I could hear from what others were saying that Jesus of Nazareth was in that crowd, and it was because of him that the people had gathered. I had heard a lot about this man. He was the subject of gossip all over the area and I don't think there can have been many folk who hadn't heard about the things he had been doing. Tales about curing incurable diseases were told wherever folk met. I wanted to meet this Jesus very badly.

So I shouted at the top of my voice to catch his attention. But immediately I was told "Oh, shut up, Bartimaus". No one wants to pay any attention to a blind man. Beggars should know their place. But I was determined - I would not shut up and I kept on shouting. And despite the efforts of his companions to hustle him on, I knew Jesus had stopped. One of these disciples came over to me and touched my shoulder. I jumped up, leaving my coat and begging bowl where they lay, and allowed myself to be led over to where Jesus stood.

Then Jesus spoke to me. It was such a daft question he asked that I couldn't believe my ears. What did I want? Wasn't it obvious? There was no hiding the fact that I was blind. But then I realised that he wanted me to ask for what I wanted. So that's what I did. I asked him to make me see. And that's exactly what I got - a life-changing moment!

The first face I ever saw was his face. A face full of love and compassion. Eyes that looked into mine and understood what I needed. A smile that spoke of joy, of acceptance into a new life full of promise.

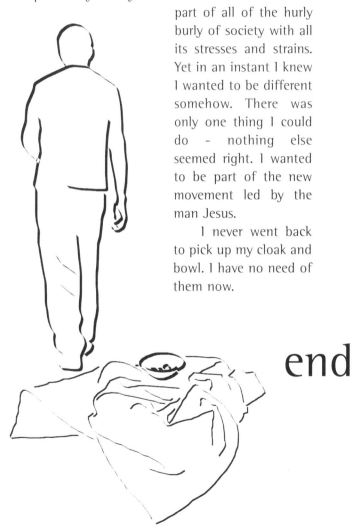

What was I going to do now? It would be scary leaving my old way of life behind. After all, I knew what each day as a beggar would bring - a mixed bag of cursing and blessing but usually enough kindness to keep body and soul together. In a way it was quite secure. Never again would I sit by the road side, let the world pass me by and rely on others to look after me. I would have to take responsibility for my own life. I would have to be a part of all of the hurly burly of society with all its stresses and strains. Yet in an instant I knew I wanted to be different somehow. There was only one thing I could do - nothing else seemed right. I wanted to be part of the new movement led by the man Jesus.

I never went back to pick up my cloak and bowl. I have no need of them now.

end

Reflection

Sometimes it seems strange to have to ask for the things we want. After all, we believe that God knows our innermost thoughts. But are we really prepared to accept the consequences of getting what we want? It can be a life-changing event for us, too, and sometimes perhaps God waits for us to be ready for this and to show this by asking.

• Spend a few moments thinking about what is happening around you and in your life. Is there something that you really want to do? Or something that you wish you could change? Try to identify some symbol that could represent what would be left behind if that change took place. You may wish to have this with you before you begin the next step or you may just want to imagine it.

Now imagine yourself standing in front of Jesus. He asks you what you want. When you hesitate he says that you must ask him to give you what you want. So you tell him. How will life change for you now? Lay down the symbol and imagine yourself walking away from it as Jesus looks into your eyes and smiles. What do you do? Will you follow where he leads or perhaps hesitate? Perhaps you are not yet quite ready for the change. Or perhaps Jesus knows this is not the right time or the right move for you.

• Spend some time relaxing in his company, just being beside him, enjoying the touch of his hand as he encourages you to be with him.

Prayer

Lord Jesus,
You call us to come to talk to you
  -sometimes we come willingly
  -sometimes we hesitate.
You ask us what we want
  -sometimes we know
  -sometimes we don't.
You wait for our answer
  -sometimes it's easy to find the words
  -sometimes it's so difficult we can only groan.
You promise to be with us always
  -sometimes you are so near we feel the loving caress of your hand
  -sometimes you seem so far away we struggle to keep you in sight.
You pledge the *shalom* that is only yours to give
  -sometimes we feel the touch of its embrace
  -sometimes we struggle even to embrace the idea.

Yet despite our hesitations and uncertainties
You remain true to your promises
You alone are the real joy-giver
You alone can save.

In our moments of doubt and despair
When we tread through desert days
Through nights of deepest darkness
never leave us or forsake us.

Open our eyes to see the beauty of life
lived in your company and in the assurance of forgiveness.
Open our eyes to see our own real needs
  and also the needs of others which require our action.
Open our eyes to see the goodness of the Father
  and the love with which we are surrounded
Open our hearts and minds to the work of the Spirit
  at work in us and in those around us.
May we, in faith, rise up
  leave behind the old, blind self
And follow you joyfully
with a new way of seeing life.
Amen

feeding the 5000 and walking on water

Matthew 14:13-26

We were absolutely exhausted that night. It had been a long, busy day despite the fact that for once we'd tried to get away from the people who kept crowding around to see Jesus. We had only just come back from our first efforts in the mission field and we had a lot to talk about. We desperately needed to rest and eat properly again. The terrible death of John the Baptist was still on our minds, and under the circumstances it seemed a good idea to keep a low profile for a while. Why does nothing happen the way it's planned?

We set off in the boat to find a deserted part of the lake shore. No people, nice and quiet - away from everything. When we arrived we found that the long walk around the lake hadn't stopped people from following us. We'd been beaten to it and there was already a crowd waiting. Of course, Jesus couldn't just ignore them, he ended up doing his usual - teaching and healing the sick folk.

It was all very well for Jesus, he was doing something useful. All we could do was watch in frustration as the crowd grew. The hours went by and we got hungrier and hungrier. My stomach began to rumble like the lake thunder! Jesus never seemed to notice time or hunger or heat or tiredness once he got involved with people and their problems. Eventually, we told him that he'd have to send everyone away to get themselves some food or they'd start getting faint! His reply seemed plain daft.

"Oh, they don't need to go away. YOU feed them."

"The sun must have got to you, Jesus. We haven't got the kind of money that feeding this lot would need. It would cost a fortune!"

"There must be some food around, just look for it."

Easy for him to say but the only things we could come up with were five loaves and two fish that a wee boy had with him. That wasn't even enough to feed ourselves.

"Just bring them to me and we'll have a picnic," Jesus said.

Everybody sat down on the grass. Jesus took the food, said a prayer, then told us to serve the people. It took us a long time but would you believe it, there was enough to give everybody as much as they wanted. Yes, I know it's difficult to take in, but that fisherman's lunch stretched to feed the whole lot and there were twelve big baskets of food left. More leftovers than starters you could say! We'd estimated around 5000 men and then there were all the women and children. Of course, they don't usually count but with Jesus, everyone counts.

    As soon as the clearing up was done, Jesus told us to get into the boat to go to Bethsaida, on the other side of the Sea of Galilee. He said he'd join us there later after he had found some peace and quiet to pray. There had been some talk among the crowd that day about kidnapping Jesus and forcing him to become their king. This was something he really didn't want so I think he had to get away quickly and keep out of their way.

As I said before, we were really tired, but we started to row. We'd only got about half-way across when the wind began to blow up strongly against us. We were all pretty miserable.

    "That's all we need. It's fine for him, nice and comfortable on shore - probably sitting on the hillside with a gentle breeze on his face."

    "Nice work if you can get it."

    "Aye, this praying's a great excuse for taking it easy."

"He needs his peace and quiet to recover after a hectic day. But what about us? We just have to get into a boat and row."

"Bad enough on a nice night but in our state, with a gale blowing against us ..."

"Fishers of men, he said - all we catch here is a cold."

You know how people grumble when they're tired and a bit cheesed off. Nothing seems fair.

The sea got really rough as the night went by. Just before dawn someone said in a small voice,

"Eh - am I seeing things? What's that over there? Doesn't look like a boat..."

"No, you're right. The shape's wrong for a sail."

"Looks more like a person."

"Dinny be daft. We're way out from land."

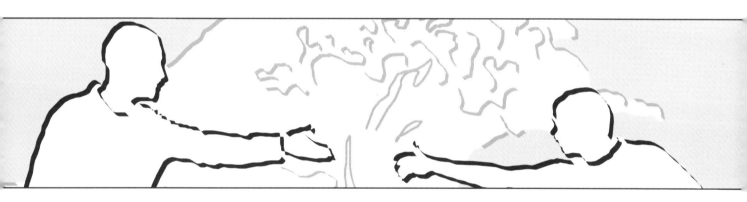

"You're seeing things."

"Must be a ghost."

"There's no such thing."

"Well if it's no' a ghost, it's a body walking on the water!"

"I don't care what it is, I'm scared."

We all were, even in the dark you could see that all our faces had gone as white as sheets. The thing came nearer ... and it was the figure of a person. It just had to be a ghost so we all started yelling at it to go away and leave us alone, but instead it spoke:

"Calm, down. What on earth's got into you? It's only me. I could see you were struggling so I've come to help."

Jesus?

Peter yelled back - you know him - speaks before he thinks.

"Well, if it's really you, tell me to walk over to you."

You can imagine the concern that caused in the boat.

"Don't be a fool, Peter. You're no' a good swimmer, man, stay where you are."

"Sit down, you're rocking the boat."

"Come on, then," said Jesus calmly.

Peter stepped over the side of the boat. Two or three of us tried to grab him but he shook us off. To our amazement he didn't immediately head for Davey Jones's locker -

he set off towards Jesus, walking on the water just like him. You could have knocked us down with a feather. He'd nearly made it when suddenly he seemed to realise what he was doing and how big the waves were. We could see him hesitate and then start to sink!

"Lord, help me, I'm drowning!" he shouted in a panic. We thought he'd had it after all. But Jesus caught his hand and held on to him as they both came towards the boat. We heard him say,

"Why didn't you trust me? You should have known I'd never ask you to do something you couldn't."

Was I right in thinking Jesus sounded really disappointed in our lack of faith in him? They climbed in beside us and to our relief the wind dropped at once and we found ourselves close to land. Looking back on what happened I suppose we shouldn't have been surprised at the things Jesus did that day, but at that time we didn't really understand much about what he said or did. And we certainly didn't know for sure who he really was.

end

Reflection

One young fisher-lad was prepared to give up all he had. It did not seem enough. The disciples did not think it would do much good yet from that offering, Jesus was able to perform a great act.

- Can you think of any stories from modern life (or history) that illustrate something similar happening? It might be someone in your community who, from personal interest or conviction, started a small campaign which grew into something big.

If the disciples had not found the lad and encouraged him to come forward with his meagre lunch the huge crowd might not have been fed. Jesus saw what could be done with something that seemed so insignificant in relation to the task. Neither the age of the giver nor the size of the gift was a barrier – the gift was welcome.

- How can we encourage each other to look for the things we might offer to share? How can we ensure that every gift, no matter how small it seems or from whom it comes, is valued and given a chance to be put to use?

Peter trusted that he could do what he was invited to do. He was prepared to try something very different, something risky. It's impossible to say why he suddenly seemed unable to carry it through. Perhaps the waves hid Jesus from his sight just for a second. Perhaps it was just the realisation of the risk he was taking. Perhaps he was seized by a terrible fear that he could not do what was expected of him.

We are told by Jesus that we will not be tried beyond our strength. Believers hold dear the idea that God will help them and give them strength to see them through the rough patches. Many people are surprised by the way they have coped with difficult circumstances. They attribute this to their faith. Some find faith as they struggle with a particularly difficult patch in life. Other people are put off by what they describe as glib phrases offered by religion.

- Have you heard phrases used that you feel could sound glib (or even offend or hurt) when people are having problems? How can we offer the Good News of the Christian faith to those who might feel this way? You may have experiences you wish to share, but do remember the importance of keeping confidential the things other people may have shared with you.

It should not always be seen as failure when that bold step out of the boat has not been successful. Peter had a personal experience that demonstrated how Jesus was prepared to come to his aid when he got into trouble. The others in the boat also saw that this happened. So they all learned something about trust from Peter's experience. We too can learn from each other's experience.

- Have there been times when you regretted taking that bold step out of the safety of the boat and needed the supporting hand of the Master to stop you from drowning? If you are working in a group, you may wish to share this experience if you feel able.

Prayer

Dear Lord,
When we hunger after the food of life
provide the banquet that will sustain our souls.
When we seek time out to pray
help us find the solitary place of peace.
When we fail to recognise your presence with us
  let recognition break through.
When the seas of life are rough
  shelter us from the storm that could overwhelm.

Amen

^ason's homecoming

Luke 15:11-32

He must have been waiting, looking out for me. He could not have met me on the road up to the house otherwise. He says he was longing for my return and each day he kept hoping it would be that day. That's not what I expected. I was sure that he would have written me off. He must have suspected that I'd turned out to be a no-good waster despite everything he had tried to do. I'd taken the money and run, glad to be shot of all the family ties that were such a pain. You know the sort of thing I mean, I'm sure. An elder brother who ruled the roost. Ordered me about no end. A father who kept hold of the purse-strings and expected such a lot from me. No freedom to do what I wanted. Always at someone's beck and call. Always too much work in the family farming business. Everyone made sure I kept my nose to the grindstone and for what? Taken for granted. Used. Nobody understood me or cared about how I felt. That's how it seemed to me when I was younger.

One day I'd had enough. I took the bull by the horns and asked for my share of the business there and then. Told Dad that I didn't want to wait till he died. After all, I might be an old man by then and too long in the tooth to make anything of it. I might even die before him! It must have hurt him, I suppose, but he agreed to give me my share. Of course, I had no intention of staying on the farm and a couple of days later I sold out and left. I went as far away as I possibly could - well out of reach of family control.

And did I have fun! You name it - I did it. Fine clothes, fine food and every luxury you care to name. The friends I made thought me a great lad. I had money to spend and I spent every penny on the good life. I did all the things I knew the family would disapprove of. But money does not last long and all too soon it was gone. Then the famine came and my so-called friends disappeared along with the food.

I had to get a job to keep myself but the only one that came along was on a pig-farm. Never could I have imagined that I would sink so low - working with the very animals that were banned as unclean. I was so hungry that the bean-pod swill that I gave to the pigs looked good enough to eat. Eventually, it dawned on me that even the servants at home had more than enough to eat. The only sensible thing to do was to go home and ask Dad if he would take me on as a hired worker. I knew I had no right to be called his son - I had lost that right through my own stupidity .

It was not an easy journey. I was hungry and dirty and desperately unsure of what Dad would do when he saw me. My thoughts were in turmoil. I had nightmares about my father pretending not to know me, refusing to talk to me, turning me away from the door. I knew I couldn't blame him if he did react like that. I would have deserved all that and more for the way I had treated him.

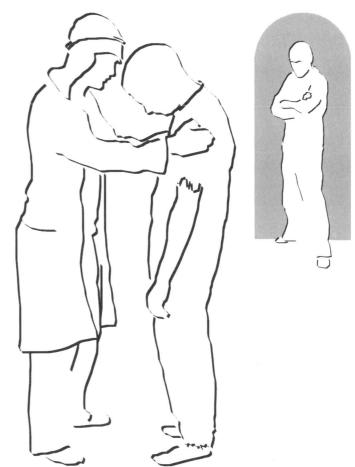

But what a surprise! He came running out and met me while I was still quite a distance from the gate. His face was red and dripping with sweat in the heat. As he flung his arms around me in a great bear-hug I could hear the breath gasping in his throat from running so hard. His welcome-home kiss spoke louder than any words. I was still his son. I mattered.

I couldn't believe it, but I was determined to say what I came to say. I told him that I knew I had been wrong and I didn't deserve to be called his son. It was difficult to speak for the lump in my throat and before I could go any further and ask to be given a job as a servant he had taken over. He shouted orders right, left and centre. Servants were rushing about bringing a fine cloak, a ring and shoes. These are not things that you give to servants. They were gifts for a person of worth.

Now one of the greatest gifts is the gift of hospitality and if someone you respect a lot comes to visit, you give a great feast for them. We always kept a specially bred, well fed calf for such an occasion. Dad ordered it to be killed and roasted to celebrate my coming home. He said he felt as if I'd come back to life after being dead or had been lost and was found again. So the party began.

During all this kerfuffle my elder brother had been working in a field away from the house and missed the excitement. When he came close enough to hear the music he asked what was going on. He was furious when he heard that my return was the cause of the fuss and he refused to come into the house. Dad went out to him and tried to explain, begging him to come and join in the celebrations. It was no good. Now it was his turn to feel unappreciated. You should have heard him. Of course, he was right when he said he had always done what he was expected to do, always obeyed orders, working all hours to keep the business profitable. He had done all this, been a good son, one a father could be proud of and for what? He had never even been given a cheap goat to give a party for his friends! He was right to accuse me of wasting my inheritance and behaving as no respectable young man would do. He resented the fact the prize calf had been killed for me, when I did not deserve that respect. A party for someone who had brought only disgrace to the family name – what was there to celebrate in that?

Dad's reply was that everything he owned belonged to my brother and that they should celebrate because my return to the family was like a return from the dead. He was celebrating the return of something precious that had been lost to him. I've never been convinced that my brother came to accept that fully and to understand what my return home meant to Dad. I often wonder if he still holds a grudge about what happened. We don't talk about it now. All I know is that I came to understand what a father's love can mean when it is so freely given. I came to understand what forgiveness really is when it's given with such generosity.

end

Music

Common Ground 36 - 'Forgiveness is your gift'

Questions to think about

While the story focuses on the forgiving love of the father for the child who has gone astray, it also speaks to us about how we respond to such situations.

- What might the elder brother have felt when his brother made demands on their father, then sold up and left home?
- What do you think the elder brother felt when his brother came back? If the father had acted differently, do you think the elder brother would have responded differently?
- What specific acts of the father would have affected the elder brother most, do you think?

Accepting that this story illustrates God's love for his children, there are times when the Christian family (define that as you will) may be reluctant to join in the celebration when a prodigal returns.

- Can you identify a situation when this has happened either in your own experience or within the wider Christian community?
- Is there any similarity between the feelings that were identified in the first question when you thought about the elder brother and any feelings that may have been at work in this situation?
- How can we help each other to overcome these feelings?

Prayer

Father God,
You love each of us as your child
Yet we sometimes long to be free of the demands you make.
You offer us only the best
Yet we run and seek fulfilment elsewhere.

Creator God,
We are made in your likeness
Yet we find it difficult to act as you act.
You show us love in all its splendour and generosity
Yet we reflect only a dimly flickering flame

Forgiving God
You wipe away the sins of those who truly repent
Yet we store up indictments against others
You charge us to forgive others as we ourselves are forgiven
Yet we often find that is a trial that is too difficult

Loving God
Through the ages you have never given up on us
Shine your light into the darkest corners of our hearts
Help us accept that your forgiveness received by others
Is as genuine and valid as that we receive ourselves.
Our Father in heaven
Help us to be your loving family here on earth.
In your holy name we pray,
Help us do your will
For yours is the kingdom, the power and glory
Now and for ever

Amen

down by the riverside

Matthew 3:1-17; Mark 1:1-11

It was quite a spectacle that day, down by the riverside. Over the past few weeks folk had gathered from far and near, keen to find out if the old prophesy was indeed being fulfilled. Hundreds of people came each day to hear the words of the stranger, hoping the wait was over.

For over 400 years we had not heard the voice of a prophet. God had been silent. Well, that's what we thought. No one had used the well known phrase 'This is what the Lord says'. No call to live as the people of God were supposed to live. No one to condemn the way we were living. No one to remind us of God's laws. Nothing. Just centuries of silence. Centuries of doing our own thing. Oh yes, there was the usual teaching by the religious men but somehow they just seemed to be looking back to see what what others - the old prophets like Isaiah, Micah and Amos - meant for today. There were no new voices, no new ideas to right the wrongs that we could see all around us.

But in one way it didn't matter all that much. The wrongs in our society were much the same as they had been all those centuries ago. A religion divided - Pharisees and Sadducees bickering about practice and doctrine - Zealots seeing violent political action as a means of getting what they wanted - the weak and vulnerable ignored or oppressed by those in power. Individuals searching for fulfilment in material things rather than in the ways of God. All in all, the people of God failing to live as the people of God should, just as they had done from time to time down though the ages. History repeating itself.

But now something was different. Was God once again speaking to us? Offering a way back through grace rather than taking revenge on the renegades? We Jews as a nation and as individuals lived with the expectation that some day, the Son of God would come among us and sort everything out. The Kingdom of God would be here on earth. Not pie-in-the-sky-when-you-die stuff but here and now - the man to be called the Messiah would be in the flesh, among us in the daily toil of life, making real a kingdom where God reigned and God's laws where obeyed. We also knew that before that could happen, a messenger would arrive to give us time to get ready. Well, things were in such a mess that they would need to be sorted out before that could happen!

Word usually went out in advance of the visit of the King to an area. The ordinary roads were just dirt tracks designed for donkeys and could not take carriages. Even the special road, the King's Highway, had to be repaired before the visit. So preparing for a King was something we knew about from experience. It was important to be ready - no community wanted to be found ill prepared as that would demonstrate a lack of respect and the consequences would not be pleasant! The prophet Isaiah had spoken of a voice from the wilderness that would come to prepare the way of the Lord. So when a man did come out of the wilderness preaching about the coming of the Messiah, it was not unexpected.

John was about thirty years old. Some thought him just another eccentric, others openly called him a nutcase. (We'd seen his like before hadn't we?) The camel hair tunic belted round his waist was hardly the height of fashion even among the lowliest shepherds! And his eating habits were strange too - wild honey and locusts didn't feature hugely in the diet of normal folk! But we discovered that his life style was modelled on that of Elijah, and he had been such an important prophet that God had taken him up to heaven in a whirlwind when he died. We remembered that the Messiah's herald was often called the second Elijah. So John seemed to fit the job description pretty well.

And when John started preaching, his words were challenging to say the least. He accused us of relying on our ancestry to be in God's good books. As descendants of Abraham we thought that we had no need to follow the faith of our ancestors - we could just reap the rewards of their faithfulness. We had no need to heed God's rules to benefit from his love. Not good enough, John said. How wrong we were to think that, he told us all. The stones at our feet were fitter recipients of God's grace than we were.

The look on the faces of the religious leaders when he called them 'a brood of snakes' was priceless! What an insult! He seemed to have no fear about telling things as they really were. Prophets in the past made few friends and neither did John. The priests certainly did not like what he was saying. But it was pointing the finger at Herod the Governor for marrying his brother's wife that would be John's undoing, and eventually he died a horrible death for that.

John kept saying that the Kingdom of God was indeed coming soon and that we needed to be ready for it. Echoes of what prophets had said down through the ages were being heard again. Everyone had to turn away from wrong thinking and acting. To turn to God and behave as the people of God should behave. We had to repent, be truly sorry for what we had done, and show it in the way we lived. Not empty words but actions - that is what repentance really means.

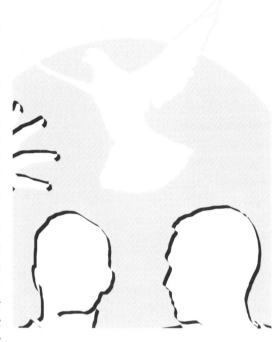

I for one did not fancy the repercussions of disobeying that call! The picture of God taking an axe and cutting down and burning every tree that did not bear good fruit certainly made me stop and think. I had been there on several occasions to hear what John said. I had been there when he had said that to avoid being destroyed everyone who has two shirts must give one to the man who has none and whoever has food must share it. I had been there when the tax collectors asked what they should do and had been told to collect only what is legal. I had heard him tell the soldiers to be content with their pay and not force anyone to give them money or to blame anyone for things they hadn't done.

John's powerful preaching hit hard and hit home. However, while he left us in no doubt that God was angry and could take a terrible revenge, John also gave us a message of hope. The good news was that those who repented would be saved. Those who repented could be baptised. To immerse someone in water as a sign of change had been accepted for long enough - anyone becoming a Jew would have been expected to go through this rite. So hundreds of people were baptised by John as a sign that they had repented. Day after day the crowds gathered and more and more people accepted his call to come to a proper relationship with God. More and more people prepared themselves for the coming of the long-awaited King. There was something special about all this happening down by the River Jordan. The river symbolised the boundary of the Promised Land, so crossing it could be seen as the point of transition before people could enter into God's promises. The Jordan was a symbol of change, a place of leaving things behind and moving on into a whole new life full of promise. A place of transformation. To bring that together with the act of baptism was very powerful.

We all knew that this man was special and we began to wonder if John was the Messiah. But he soon stopped that rumour. The Messiah was still to come. John likened himself to a slave who was too humble even to fasten his master's sandals. He said that he baptised with water but the Messiah would baptise by fire, a baptism that would be spiritual as well as symbolic. He had no doubt that the Messiah was mightier than himself and this baptism would be of the Holy Spirit.

Anyway, all that had happened before the day that will live with me until the day I die. It all started off pretty normally. The call to repent, the promise of God to forgive and John standing in the water to perform the baptisms just as usual. Someone pointed out to me a young man from Nazareth among the crowd. He was about the same age as John and I was told that they were cousins. When this man, whose name was Jesus, stepped down the gravel bank and into the river to be baptised John did not seem too happy about the idea. He seemed to think that Jesus did not need to submit to a baptism that signified repentance. I think he knew all along who Jesus was although the rest of us didn't. John knew that Jesus had not committed any sins - why did he want to be baptised? Perhaps Jesus felt that in his case baptism was a sign that he was prepared to submit to the demands that God would make of him. Perhaps it was a marking of his dedication to his ministry and mission.

Jesus had come up out of the water and was standing there dripping wet when it happened. Above our heads the blue of the sky seemed to open up so that we could see far beyond. Just a tantalising glimpse - was it heaven? Slowly a dove flew down, fluttered gracefully around him for a few moments then landed on his hand. That in itself seemed like an omen. The dove, a symbol of peace and of gentleness coming down from heaven to earth. You could see folk looking at each other, wondering. This had not happened to anyone else. What could it mean? We soon found out. A voice came from heaven saying, "This is my son, whom I love; with him I am well pleased.". God's voice speaking to us at long last. God's voice speaking directly to God's people, telling us that the Messiah had arrived. God's voice telling the world that it was about to be turned upside down.

As we went home that day, there was a feeling that something tremendous had happened. Somehow we knew that things would never be the same again and we had been part of a new beginning.

end

Questions to consider

For the first two questions, if working with a group you may want to use a 'silent wall' to record your thoughts or have a 'buzz', then the leader can make a list on a flip-chart.

Imagine what would happen if John the Baptist appeared on the banks of the Forth or Clyde or Dee or Spey or a river that runs close to where you live.

• What would John say about how he found that community? Would he find people living out their lives as the people of God? Identify some of the things that you think he might criticise, things that could be seen as contrary to the will of God? Feel free to look wider than your own community if you feel this is appropriate – after all, John was speaking to a wider audience than just those who lived beside the Jordan!

Remember that every community has things happening within it on which it might be said that God will be smiling.

• What might these be?

John spoke of the coming of the Kingdom of God. Jesus spoke many times of the same concept. While the full realisation of this may not come while we are in this world, there is a sense in which it is already with us. In thinking about preparing ourselves as subjects of that kingdom, what values might we need to be prepared to accept?

• What 'rules' would you see as essential for those who would live in that Kingdom as it is fulfilled here on earth?

• Write a Constitution (up to ten rules for citizens) for the Kingdom of God. You might find it helpful to consider this by using a formula such as 'Every citizen of the Kingdom will have the right to ... and therefore will have a responsibility to ...'

Unlike Jesus, all of us fall short of the God's demands on our way of life.

• Which of the rules that you have decided are important do you think will be most difficult to keep? If you are working in a group it is necessary to recognise that this question could be a difficult one for people to address. Discussion in any depth may not be appropriate, especially if people are just beginning to get to know and trust each other. You may decide to keep it on a very general level - using terms such as 'people' rather than 'you'– and look at the church or community rather than from individual perspective.

Music

CH3 208 - 'On Jordan's bank the Baptist's cry announces that the Lord is nigh'
Common Ground 28 - 'Comfort, comfort now my people'
Songs of God's People 101 - 'The God of heaven is present on earth'

Prayer

God of humankind,
You are our maker and sustainer
In gratitude we recognise your goodness
In love we come to seek out your will
In lives dedicated freely to working for the coming of your Kingdom
Seeking your strength to do what is needed
Lord of life, we come to you.

Amen

the taxman up a tree

Luke 19:1-9; Mark2:13-17

I never really liked crowds. All that jostling was just too much. Sometimes folk took advantage of the pushing and shoving to push me particularly hard. And there were all those sarcastic, cutting comments that people meant me to overhear. Jibes about taxmen and cheats. And about my height. I'd grown used to it, but they still hurt. I liked to think that I began to act the way I did because of the way people jeered. A sort of retaliation, I suppose. If they didn't look up to me in one way they'd have to in another. That's how I hit back. I had power and I'd used it to bring me wealth, but it never gave me the respect I so much yearned for. Wherever I went I was recognised, pointed out and punished for what I was and what I did. Anyway, in a crowd, I never could see what was going on unless I could push my way to the front and that didn't often happen. So between that and the victimisation I learned to avoid crowds. No one with any sense chooses such abuse.

Sometimes being short meant that I missed things and one day something was happening that I was determined not to miss. Word had come that Jesus was coming into town. Jericho was buzzing with the news and I knew that everybody would want to see him. I'm still not sure why it was so important to me to see him too. Deep down inside I just felt it was something I had to do - something calling me I suppose. As I thought about it I remembered the big sycamore tree that grew beside the road into the town. He'd have to come that way. It wasn't far from where I worked and I managed to get there without being seen. It was a bit of a struggle but I managed to haul myself into the tree and hide away in the shade of the dense leaves. I thought Jesus would never see me there - I'd be able to see him and I'd be safe from the others too.

It wasn't long before they arrived. First the townsfolk, huddling in groups along the roadside. Then Jesus and his disciples and the groupies that gathered wherever they went. I felt really pleased with myself. I could see them all clearly and even hear what they were saying. Jesus seemed happy as he chatted away to folk as he passed. As he came closer to me I could see the dust from the long walk on his clothes and in his hair. He stopped right under the branch where I was hiding and looked up into my eyes. I knew then that there was no place that I could hide from him. I could feel my face getting red and I prayed he'd just ignore me and pass on. Then he said, "Come down, Zacchaeus". My heart missed a beat as he said my name - he knew me! But his next sentence flabbergasted me

and everyone else too. He wanted to come to my house for dinner.

To say it was an undignified scramble down from that tree is an understatement. What had been done in secret had to be undone in the full gaze of people who enjoyed my embarrassment. Feeling very silly and dishevelled I got my feet back on the ground but could hardly hold my head up. I led Jesus through that hostile crowd to my home. Even so, I was glad that Jesus had chosen to speak to me and wanted to be seen with me.

Now, as I said, I am a wealthy man. I was also known for being a good host and keeping an excellent table. That's a time-honoured way of becoming popular - buying a way into people's friendship. But of course only certain people would be seen in my company. Only those whose professions or background made every good Jewish person shun them. Those who were members of, or who carried out the wishes of, the government. Those who enforced the edicts of our Roman masters. Tax collectors are not the most popular people in any society. The Romans used local people to collect the money for them. They laid down rules about how much money they had to collect but not about how much the taxmen could take. That meant we could charge virtually what we liked and as long as we gave the Romans what they expected no questions were asked. So the more we took, the more we could keep. It wasn't difficult to get rich. Extortion backed by force from the Roman authorities (not known for their compassion) was common. I was good, very good, at playing the system - I was a Chief Inspector of Taxes. I deserved everything the people threw at me.

So that night, Jesus sat down to dine in the company of the least respected in our society. The religious leaders hated us - our dealings with the general public made us impure from a religious viewpoint so they shunned us. The people of the community hated us for the way we treated them. The Romans had little respect for us although they were prepared to use us for their own ends. To eat in such company is something no self-respecting Jew was allowed to do and the religious leaders were not slow in coming forward to criticise Jesus. Why did he lower himself to eat with such a group?

Jesus' reply showed that he felt there was a job to be done among the likes of us. Our relationships with our fellow human beings needed doctoring just as much as those whose lameness or blindness were physical signs of ill-health. Our relationship with God had been damaged by the way we treated others and we needed help to begin to heal the wounds, both self-inflicted and inflicted on others.

I knew what I had to do. To start with, I decided to give half my large fortune to the poor. Then I had to pay back all the extra money I had collected and pay it back with interest. So I decided there and then to pay everyone four times the amount I had I cheated from them. Jesus recognised that I had realised how wrong I had been. He said that it was folk like me whom he had come to save.

I'm not sure that anyone will ever look up to me now, but I'm glad that I couldn't hide from Jesus that day. Answering Jesus's call to walk beside him was a life changing experience and I wouldn't have missed it for all the money in the world. One thing I learned that evening was that the important thing is not the job that you do, it's the way that you do it that matters. The riches Jesus promises are worth far more than anything that money can buy.

end

Reflections

- Can you think of some people who use power today in a way which is damaging to others?
- Like Zacchaeus, they may try to justify what they do. What reasons might they put forward (e.g. bombing is necessary to counteract or discourage terrorism)?
- Are there ways in which we collude with them in allowing these actions to take place? How can we as Christians make our feelings known if we don't agree with what is done?
- That evening at Zacchaeus's dinner table, one of the main topics of conversation must have been the way people treat each other. Imagine what might happen if Jesus came to your church (or community or group or home). What topic(s) would he want to discuss with you and what do you think he would say? Is there anything that needs to be 'healed'?

You may find Psalm 134 appropriate as an additional reading.

Music

CH368 - 'Thou art before me Lord. Thou art behind' is based on Psalm 134. Sing it to the tune 'Highland Cathedral'.

Prayer

Lord of every part of our life,
Before we were made you knew us.
No mountain is high enough,
No sea deep enough
To hide us from you.

Every road we walk you are by our side
No twist or turn
No pothole, no matter how deep
Can take us from your sight.

Every task we do we should do as for you
No job is too insignificant
No circumstance too difficult
To seek your help to tackle.

When life gets tough and we falter
No strength to do the thing we should
No courage to face the hostile crowd
Your right hand will hold us fast.

If power abuses or corrupts and
No voice defends the vulnerable
No action aids the weak
Your people need to hear you call.

Then let us in answer say
Yes, and work to put right the wrong. Say
Yes, and seek to do your will
Lead us in the way everlasting, O lord.

Amen

peter's piece

Acts 10

I liked staying with Simon the tanner. He had a house in Joppa, just up from the harbour. I had got into the habit of going up on to the roof there to say my prayers. Even in the hottest part of the day there was a bit of a cool sea breeze blowing up there and it was away from the dust of the street too.

One day about noon I went up on the roof and settled comfortably to pray. But not long after I started (and I often went on for quite a while) I began to feel hungry. It was a long time since breakfast and I'd had a busy morning, so food seemed like a good idea. I called down to the women and asked them to bring me a 'piece' (that's what we called bread and cheese in my part of the world). Then I went back to my prayers.

But then a strange thing happened. I had a sort of waking dream - you might call it a vision. Down from the sky came a sheet, slung by its four corners. In the sheet were things which wriggled and things which writhed, so that the sheet heaved and swayed. It was lowered to the ground, and I saw that it was full of all kinds of animals, reptiles and wild birds. And then a voice from nowhere said, "Peter, get up from your knees. Stop dreaming about all the things you might have. Choose something from this lot, kill it, cook it and put it in your piece."

Of course, I was absolutely horrified because in the sheet were all sorts of things that I, as a good Jew, could not possibly eat. All my life I had been taught that certain things were unclean and that it was against God's law to eat them. Snakes and pigs and some wild birds and things that lived in the sea but didn't have fins and scales were forbidden. Not allowed. Not under any circumstances. So I said,

"Not me, God knows I've never eaten a bacon butty in my life!"

"Just do as you are told," came the reply. "Kill and eat. Nothing that God has made is unclean."

But I was adamant and replied,

"I know ostrich burgers are very popular with the in-crowd but that sort of thing will never pass my lips!"

"I'm telling you that it's OK - enjoy some prawn cocktail. Nothing God has made is unclean."

"Not on your life. I've never broken the law about what is allowed to eat and I'm not about to start now."

And with that the sheet and all the curious animals it contained was hoisted back up into the sky and out of sight.

Now I was really puzzled. I knew the law. I knew which animals were allowed for eating and which were not. It was something that every Jewish boy and girl grew up knowing about. It was bred into us. It was one of the things which distinguished us from every other nation around. It was a way we had of making sure we kept on the right side of God; something which set us apart as God's people.

While I was trying to make sense of all this, there was a knock at the door. Three men were there asking if this was where someone called Simon Peter was staying (that's my full Sunday name!) Just as they arrived I heard that voice say,

"I sent these men to find you. Go with them, you have a job to do."

So I went down from the roof and introduced myself and asked "Why are you here?" And this was the story they told me.

They came from a man called Cornelius who was Captain of a Roman regiment but who worshipped God. He was well known and liked by the Jewish community in a town called Caesarea. Cornelius had also had a vision. In his vision an angel had told him about me, where I was staying and that he was to invite me to visit him. So Cornelius sent three servants to find me.

We all set off the next morning for Caesarea. Some of my Christian friends from Joppa came with us. It took us all day to walk there and

when we arrived at Cornelius's house we were surprised to see a crowd of his relatives and close friends all waiting for us.

And that's the end of the story. It seems a bit tame really. No dramatic miracle like raising someone from the dead or laying on a feast for the crowd from a wee boy's picnic lunch. No big deal. Or was it?

You see, for the people waiting in that house it was quite an experience. None of them was born a Jew, although some of them did worship the Jewish God and might even have kept the laws about what to eat. But still they were not accepted as 'proper' Jews. Very inferior. Proper Jews would not mix freely with them in company. And in that crowd were folk that worshipped other gods. And there were Romans too. Definitely not the sort of company any self-respecting Jew would keep. At that time, anyone who wasn't a Jew was called a Gentile, so the world was divided into two classes of people - Jews and Gentiles.

And of course, I was a good, self-respecting, God-fearing Jew. So to be seen in such company was questionable. To go into such a house was unthinkable. To be friends with a Gentile who was considered to be unclean would make you unclean too. To eat from dishes that had been contaminated by unclean food would be a sin. And there were lengthy rituals that would need to be gone through to make a person clean again and acceptable into Jewish society. So even to go inside that house was to go against everything that my religious training had taught me. But that's what I did. I went in, and I stayed under that roof. It was just something that had to be done.

As I explained to them, "You know that no Jew is allowed to be friends with Gentiles. At least that's what our religion has taught us in the past. But now God has told me that I must not think about people being unclean. There is no difference in God's eyes between us simply because of where we have been born or the way we have been brought up. This is the Good News that Christ has brought."

I had to explain that in order to obey God, I had to change my mind about things I had been brought up to believe were important to God. It wasn't easy but I had been shown that this was how things must be. If I hadn't obeyed I would have missed the opportunity to spread the Good News that God's love is for everyone. So that day friends and I had to put aside our old prejudices and show love in real action.

Of course, I got into trouble for doing it. Some of my friends back home didn't approve one little bit of me sitting down to tuck into prawn cocktails with my new-found friends. They even ... but that's another story!

end

Reflection

Simon Peter believed that eating certain food was sinful, and that there were people in the world who were to be shunned. These beliefs were part of his religious teaching. Such teaching had made Peter prejudiced against part of God's creation.

- What would you find shocking if someone told you to do it? Take time to think about some examples and why you feel this way about them.

- What do you recognise as a prejudice? It could be something personal or it could be something that comes from the church.

- What is as unacceptable to you as a pig was for Peter? What has wrapped this up and tied it so securely in your mind?

With a group

- Give everyone a small piece of pink paper with a pig outline on it. Ask people to hold the pig in their hands as they listen to some music. They think about their prejudices, and if they wish, write them on the pig. The pigs will be collected later and pinned on a flip-chart or notice board. This will be quite anonymous, and no one need feel they have to write anything down.
- Play track 5 from 'O God you search me and you know me' (from 'Christ be our Light' – Bernadette) while people are thinking and writing.

- Pass round the basket to collect the pigs and pin them up.
- Have a discussion about the prejudices – where did they come from? What made people change their minds about them? Have the pigs 'flown'?
  (Miracles do happen!)

Prayer

Creator God
In love you challenge us
To love each other despite ourselves.
Blow through our lives with the breath of life.
That reveals your truth and challenges each of us to be open to it..
Blow through your church like a gale
Blowing away the dust of outworn traditions;
Where we have become tangled in cobwebs of prejudice
Sweep them away to reveal the true beauty of
human nature
Both in others and ourselves.
Untie the strings that bind our parcels.
Help us sort the contents and accept the surprises that are awaiting us.
From the cowardice that does not face new truths
From the laziness that is content with half truths
From the arrogance that thinks it knows all the truths
Deliver us today and every day good Lord.

Amen

an act of
devotion

John 12:1-11

It was six days before the Passover that he came back to our house in Bethany. Only a couple of weeks before, he'd been with us and since then things had got much more tense. Raising my brother Lazarus from the dead had been a very public act and many of the people who heard about that now believed that Jesus was the Messiah. Of course, the Jewish authorities didn't like that one bit and were even more determined to get rid of him. The crowds that moved along the roads leading to Jerusalem for the celebrations were told to be on the lookout for him. He was a wanted man.

Looking back, I think the disciples were unsure of what would happen. Some had tried to persuade him not to come, but they still supported him when he refused to take their advice. Some of them, I'm sure, got a kick from the sense of danger that was all around. I don't think they accepted the fact that Jesus was heading for arrest and execution. Surely this great cause that they believed in and had devoted months of their life to could not come to such a tragic end? Certainly they did know that a plot was afoot to kill Jesus (and Lazarus too) but I think they had a vision of an army of angels with flaming swords descending from heaven to take over Jerusalem, depose the government and install Jesus as king.

The men were sitting around the table talking and eating just as they always did, when something came over me. As usual, everyone's feet had been washed before they sat down but no oil had been poured over their heads to remove the dust. Often this was done by the host rather than a servant and I suppose we'd just been too busy to get round to doing it. Suddenly it was very important to me that this was done for Jesus. As I went to get the oil I realised that there was something very special about this occasion and the ordinary oil did not seem good enough. So I fetched the spikenard that had come all the way from the Himalayas. It had cost a fortune and was very precious. So precious that it was sealed into a beautifully made alabaster flask. It seemed the only appropriate oil to anoint the man who was so precious to me.

The atmosphere round the table was strange. The joy that we had at being together again was tinged with a sense of foreboding. Seeing Lazarus there, full of life, reminded everyone how much we owed Jesus. Yet we knew we were harbouring a wanted criminal and that he had arrived openly. Would one of our neighbours or one of the many pilgrims passing through the village report that to the authorities? What would the repercussions be for us? When and how would the authorities act?

The men paid no attention to me as I walked into the room. I suppose they thought I was just keeping to the usual role of women at such a time and bringing in another plate of food. Martha had been in and out several times helping to serve the meal we had prepared. As I broke the neck of the flask and began to pour out the oil the fragrance drifted around the room and all attention turned to me. Kneeling there in front of our master I knew this would be the last time I would be able to show him what I felt. To wash the feet of a guest was the task of a servant, not a family member. But I wanted to show him that I was prepared to do that for him. I had already defied convention by joining the company of men at the dinner table but I could not bring myself to speak. What

could I say anyway? It is so difficult to express deep feelings - especially when you don't fully understand what is happening within yourself. My actions were speaking louder than any words could.

I could feel the sense of shock growing as I removed my veil and used my hair to wipe the oil off the feet of Jesus. No respectable woman would let a man other than her husband see her hair that way. But it felt right to do it as a sign of my total submission to Jesus. There was no way to reseal the flask, so everything in it had to be given there and then and nothing held back.

I was sure then that Jesus was walking towards his death and I couldn't understand why he was so determined to do this. I knew that he was prepared to give up his life and I needed to show him that I knew this. I knew then that he was going to die and there was nothing any of us could do to save him. I didn't understand why this was his destiny, why God had planned this all along. I just knew that Jesus knew his death was near and that he accepted the Cross as a necessary part of the plan. I used the oil that had been bought ready to embalm someone in the family to anoint Jesus before his death. There was a coldness deep down inside me as I realised that what I was doing was usually done to a corpse.

The atmosphere was heavy with the strong, sweet fragrance which is intended to mask the smell of death. It filled the house of the living. Somehow it seemed to whisper of things which no one understood and feared to voice. My tears mingled with the oil as I touched the warm flesh of Jesus's feet and I shuddered at the thought of what would happen to him soon. I understood that it was his great love for his fellow human beings that would lead Jesus's to his death. I needed to show him that I understood this, and shared something of his pain.

Into the stillness came the commotion. No one criticised me for the way I had burst into their company, for the breaking of conventions. Perhaps it came as no surprise - I'd done enough of that before when I neglected my duties as the sister of the host. It was the waste of money which became the focus. I suppose I can see the point they were trying to make. The normal wage for a day's labour was a silver denarius, and if the perfume had been sold it would have fetched nearly a year's wages. Judas said that if it had been sold more money could have been given to the poor - something accepted by Jews as an act of piety. But we knew Judas - he was always keen to have plenty of money in the kitty so that he could take what he wanted from it. How often selfish ends are disguised as points of principle.

But Jesus understood what I had done. He said that the poor would always be with us but that I had acted because I knew that he would not be with us for much longer. I had done what I could for him before his death - something that I would not be able to do after he was dead. He knew that my extravagance came out of love. He knew that love led to the sacrifice of everything precious, even life itself. He accepted my gift of love and he would not let others criticise me for what I had done.

I know now that his death would come to mean more to the poor than a gift of mere money ever could. His suffering and death would bind him to the needy and suffering folk of the world in a way nothing else could. At the time, though, all I knew was that my life had to be devoted to this man. I had recognised Jesus for who and what he was and I had shown him that I had accepted all that was to follow. Although I was afraid of what would happen to us all, I felt that somehow things would work out just as God had planned.

end

Questions for consideration

Mary was prepared to defy the conventions of her society, many of which revolved around her gender, to show her devotion in public to Jesus.

- Can you think of any conventions or attitudes that might inhibit an individual from expressing feelings?. You might find it helpful to think about the way we label people – such as 'disabled' or 'addict' or 'too young/old'.
- In your experience, how are such people actually treated when they attempt to demonstrate commitment? Does the church accept that they may do so in unexpected ways?
- Are you happy with this or would you like to see things change?
- What excuses are used to justify any criticisms made of them or their actions?
- How do you think Jesus would respond to the situation?

If you have identified matters that cause concern, try to focus on one and find a way to address it. You may wish to come back to others later.

At a personal level, is there something that is 'precious' to you that you feel you could give to Jesus as a sign of your commitment? It might be an ability rather than something with monetary value. How do you think those around you would respond to this gesture were you to make it?

Music

CH3 87 - 'Be thou my vision, Oh Lord of my heart'
CH3 462 - 'Take my life and let it be consecrated Lord to thee'
CH3 458 - 'Lord of all good our gifts we bring to thee'

Prayer

You might like to have a candle ready to light at the appropriate point in the prayer to symbolise giving your individual gift. If you are working in a group you could make the shape of a cross with the candles.

Lord Jesus,
In Mary of Bethany we see mirrored your self-giving love.
She understood as no one else did where you were going.
In wholehearted obedience to your Father's will
Your love led you to the suffering of the Cross.

In your obedience
You gave us yourself,
God's gift of God's self
Given to humankind in love,

Mary gave the most precious thing she had
Help us to follow her example of uncalculated devotion.
In wholehearted obedience to our Father's will
Give all we have in response to the covenant of the Cross.

In our obedience
We would give of ourselves.
In response to God's love
Show others love in action.

SILENCE

(Light a candle to symbolise your gift.)

Lord Jesus,
Accept our gifts and our devotion
Fill our lives and the lives of all around us
with the fragrance of your everlasting love.

Amen

palm sunday

Matthew 21:1-11, Mark 11:1-10; Luke 19:28-38; John 12:12-19

The whole area was really crowded. All around the city tents had appeared - the pilgrims were doing their self-catering bit. Lots of people had already arrived. Everyone tried to get to Jerusalem for Passover. It was the biggest festival of the Jewish year, when people remembered how God helped the Jews to escape from slavery in Egypt[1]. So the tourist season was in full swing and everybody was out to enjoy the celebrations as well as do their religious duty. It was like a family wedding only much, much bigger. Some relatives and friends met only at these events, and of course there were those who didn't come very often because they lived so far away. So you can imagine how excited the crowds were. There was pushing and jostling but it was all good-natured - nobody wanted to spoil their best clothes!

This year was different, though. There was an extra buzz going around. The folk who knew all about it (you always get some like that don't you?) were busy telling anyone who would listen. Some had already heard rumours and wanted to know more - all the gossips were having a great time. Some were already convinced that something big was going to happen soon. Some people couldn't or wouldn't believe that one man could change their world, but they still listened to those who did. Yes, they were all talking about Jesus.

Many people had seen and heard Jesus do wonderful things over the past few years - or they knew someone who had! I was one of them. I'd been there, I mean. Jesus changed my life when we met on the road near Jericho. Every day I still marvel that I can see. 'Blind as Bartimaeus' was what people used to say - not any more now that Jesus has given me my sight! I was with the crowd that followed him into Jerusalem, so I can truly say that I've seen what was happening. The disciples were there too, of course, and they seemed tense, as if they were expecting trouble any minute. Not surprising really because we all knew that the authorities had it in for Jesus. They were terrified that one way or another he might be the spark that lit the fire of revolution.

I think Jesus had stayed the night at Bethany with Lazarus and his sisters, Mary and Martha. Anyway, that morning he set off up the road towards Jerusalem. We followed on behind his close friends. Two of them left the group and went off towards another village. When they met up with us again, they were not alone. With them was a donkey and her foal. Jesus went over and spoke gently to the animals. You could tell the donkey was nervous and a wee bit skittish. Somebody said that she had never been ridden and with all the noise around the poor animal must have been really scared. But the next thing we knew was that the disciples laid cloaks on her back and Jesus got on as calm as you like and set off along the road.

This took some people by surprise. They had expected the Messiah to arrive like a mighty soldier, leading an army to rid the land of the invading Romans. And here, instead of a magnificent, strong war-horse was an ordinary donkey, the humble beast we all used to carry everyday loads like wood and hay. What was it all about?

But other folk remembered that sometimes great people rode on donkeys to show they came in peace, not war, and some remembered how the prophets had said the Messiah would ride on just such a humble animal[2]. How excited they got! Soon they were singing on their way into the Holy City. It was a new song, something different from the psalms they usually sang. They were chanting: "Praise to the Son of David. Blessings on him who comes in the name of the Lord. Praise God. Hosanna."

Then people began to cut branches from the palm trees along the roadside, and to lay them on the road. They threw their cloaks on the ground to make a carpet. The whole road was lined with crowds. It was like a royal procession and for the first time, Jesus went along with all the fuss. He didn't try to stop the people calling him 'Son of David'. Right into the city he rode like a king. Complete with thousands of followers. What a commotion! And the things that happened after that - but that's another story.

I never thought I'd see the day that our Saviour would arrive in Jerusalem. But then I never thought I'd be able to see anything! Talking about seeing things - have you ever noticed the mark on a donkey's back? If you look carefully you can see there the dark pattern of a cross. It reminds us that ordinary things and ordinary people can do wonderful things for God.

end

Notes

1 Exodus 12:1-28

2 Zechariah 9:9

Reflection

Additional material

You may wish to use the poem 'The Donkey' by
G K Chesterton

Music

CG 110 - 'Shine, Jesus, shine'
CG 82 - 'Mallaig Sprinkling Song'
SoGP 2 - 'A new commandment'
SoGP 29 - 'For the healing of the nations'
CH3 234 - 'Ride on, ride on in majesty'
CH3 235 - 'Hosanna in the highest'

When Jesus rode into Jerusalem on the back of donkey he
did something that was expected by the Jews of the
person who was to be their Messiah. It revealed his
identity to the public. As a result of his actions people
were able to see that God's promise had been kept. The
crowds were excited, full of hope that life would be
changed by the arrival of the Son of God. The herald of a
new age had arrived.

Two thousand years on and still we long for peace,
yearn for a world where each person is treated as a
person made in the image of God, hunger for justice. Two
thousand years on and it is the disciples of Christ who,
with the power of the Holy Spirit at work within them
and around them, are charged with revealing to the world
the love of God at work in the world.

When Jesus revealed his identity to those expectant
crowds he opened himself to abuse. The jeers and insults
and personal suffering that came his way were
demanding yet he kept to the path he knew he must

follow. For some Christians today life holds much danger
but for most of us, at least in the western world, there are
few such traumas. Yet it can still be a difficult path for us
to follow too. But if the new age is to come in all its
fullness it is the followers of Jesus who are charged with
the task of revelation.

Question and activity time

- Can you identify any signs of the Spirit at work today?
  You might like to consider this just within your own
  community or church or think of a wider picture.
- At an individual level, what 'signs' would you expect a
  disciple of Christ to display? Think not so much about
  symbols like wearing a cross or a fish, but think more
  about love in action
- How difficult is it to be identified openly as a Christian
  in your community? What do others expect of you if
  you admit to this? Are their expectations realistic?
- Divide into small groups to write a prayer about
  Christian witness.

Prayer

Lord Jesus,
As you used a humble donkey
To reveal to others yourself as God's Son
Use us as your humble servants
Charged with the task of making others your disciples
And loving others as you love us
Be with us always, to the end of the age.

Amen

mary's
tale

John 20:1-18

I must have looked a pretty sight. I'm not one of those women who can cry and remain elegant. No, my eyes go red and puffy and my nose runs! And I had been crying off and on for three days. So you can imagine how I looked. Or perhaps it's best not to imagine that at all!

That Friday seemed to bring the end of all we had hoped for. Our friend and master had been betrayed by one of his own companions. He had been humiliated, flogged and crucified after a mockery of a trial. He had died in agony. We couldn't bear to watch, but we couldn't not, either. There wasn't even time to bury him properly because it was almost the Sabbath by the time Joseph of Aramathea got permission to take him down from the cross. It had to be Joseph - no one else could have gone to Pilate without fear of being arrested too. Joseph was on the Council, and only a few of us knew he secretly supported Jesus. Nicodemus did his best - he brought myrrh and aloes to wrap into the linen strips that by custom are wound around a body for burial. At least that was done decently. It was just lucky that Joseph, being a rich man, had a tomb ready for his own burial in a nearby garden, and the two of them put Jesus' body into that.

Saturday was a dreadful day for all of us. We were in shock. We couldn't believe that it had ended like that. All those hopes and dreams - that the Messiah had come and the Jewish nation would be saved from oppression - all gone. And to lose a very close friend in such a way - our hearts were sore. We were confused about the way forward, and we were very frightened. Frightened of that knock on the door and what it might bring. The Roman soldiers were no respecters of the Sabbath and we were well known to be supporters of Jesus. They had killed him and it might be our turn next. Behind locked doors we wept and wondered and worried. But the day passed and the knock never came.

The night dragged by until I couldn't bear it any longer. It was so awful to think that the man I loved so dearly had not been treated with proper respect in death. I made up my mind. I left the house as quietly as I could and set off to the tomb, carrying the oils and spices to anoint his body and put things right. The road was rough and in the darkness and through my tears the way seemed steeper than usual.

I hadn't really thought things through. It hadn't crossed my mind that I wouldn't be able to get into the tomb to do what I wanted to do. The stone rolled across the entrance of a tomb isn't meant to be moved easily for obvious reasons. It would have been impossible for me to do it alone. But I hadn't thought of that. I just wanted to be there. Sorrow often clouds your mind.

I don't remember much about that journey, really, until, towards dawn, I found myself in the garden. As I picked my way along the stony garden path I looked up and saw the mouth of the tomb. I froze. No stone. It had been rolled away and the tomb gaped, darker than the night. Someone had been there. Perhaps they still were there in the half-dark, waiting to see who came?

I ran. I stumbled and slipped back down that path. Somewhere I lost a sandal but I didn't notice until later. I had to tell Peter and John and the others what had happened. I knew where they'd be. You can imagine their reaction when their door was flung open and in rushed a tear-stained woman gasping out that the tomb was open, that Jesus' body had been taken away and I didn't know where. I'm sure they thought I was a bit crazy - imagining things or had gone to the wrong tomb. They all stared at me for a minute then there was a babble as they tried to calm me down.

"What? What did you say?"

"Sit down, Mary, relax."
"You're getting yourself into a state."
"Come on now, Mary, you must be imagining things."
"There must be some logical explanation."

I didn't have breath to shout them down. Women aren't accepted as reliable witnesses at the best of times and this was not the best of times! It's a disgrace how so-called 'hysterical' women are easily brushed aside. But I knew what I had seen and I knew I was telling the truth. I just kept saying it over and over. Something in my voice convinced them, and John and Peter ran out to see for themselves. I followed. John got there first and hesitated outside the tomb, but Peter rushed straight in as usual.

What they saw proved I hadn't been imagining things. Jesus' body was gone. The linen cloths were folded neatly and laid on the shelf where his body must have lain. Peter and John rushed back to tell the others but I stayed on, I was loath to leave the last place where our Lord had been. I didn't think I had any more tears to cry, but I did. I looked into the tomb again, and I seemed to see two whitish figures sitting at either end of where his body had been. For some reason, I'll never know why, I wasn't at all afraid, and when one of them asked me why I was crying, I told them. Then I turned to go.

As I stood for a moment in the garden, I made out another figure nearby. It was getting lighter now, and I thought it was the gardener - well that was natural, seeing where I was. He could see I was upset, and he asked me what was wrong, and was I looking for anyone. I thought he might know who had taken Jesus' body away and where it was, so I asked him about it. We'd only exchanged a few words, but then he suddenly said my name, "Mary", and I knew - only one person, only Jesus, ever said my name like that. He always made it sound like I was special to him. He was - is - certainly special to me. I tried to hug him, but he said no, not yet - he said the most marvellous things. How he was soon going up to his father and mine, to his God and our God. He said I was to go to the others and tell them this.

I couldn't wait. I all but flew. But would they believe me this time ...?

end

Question time

- To have the truth of something you say doubted by others can be very difficult. What sort of emotions might you feel when this happens? You may have experienced this yourself at some time and feel able to share how you felt with others.

- How easy is it to work out the 'truth' in any situation? What factors might affect the way any individual sees the truth? You may like to write a short case-study in which two people view a situation very differently and come to different conclusions about where the truth lies.

- Is it always best to tell the truth?

Music

CG 117 - 'Spirit of God unseen as the wind'

Prayer

Lord Jesus,
Full of grace and truth
You came from the Father and became flesh
    and lived among humankind as witness
            to the truth of the love that holds us fast.
You are the way the truth and the life.
Risen from the confines of the dark tomb
    and alive in the early light of morning
            you speak our name as we seek you out.

Spirit of truth,
Ever with those who follow Christ
Light up our lives
    set us free by the truth you bring
            bring us into the sunlight of understanding
Illuminate the darkness of our minds
Teach us discernment
    that we may act wisely and fairly
            and always speak in love.

Living God,
We worship you in spirit and in truth
We praise you for the Gospel
    Guide us in your truth, teach us your ways
            so that we may bring that light to others.
You are indeed our loving Father:
    give us the strength of eagles
            when we meet disbelief.
Fill us with your grace and mercy:
    give us the gentleness of doves
            when truth might wound.

Amen

thomas's
tale

John 14:1-6; 20:24-29

How did I get my nickname? Well, I suppose I was always the one who needed to be convinced - needed to be sure in my own mind that something was true.

I remember that when Jesus was speaking to us all about the way he was going to die and the horrible things that would happen, I had to ask him what he meant. I needed an explanation so that I could understand. Mind you, I don't think the others understood anymore than I did but they didn't want to look foolish. It can be difficult to admit to not understanding something in front of all your friends. So it was I who asked the question. After all how could we know 'the way' when we didn't know where he was going? The answer I got must be one of the best known remarks of Jesus, 'I am the way'. Even now that's not easy to understand.

It wasn't that I was afraid to face what being a follower of Jesus meant. We all knew that he was planning to go to Jerusalem for the Passover. And we knew how dangerous that would be. Most of the other disciples tried to persuade him not to go. The Jewish authorities were out to get him and we knew that as well as he did. I realised that he was determined to go and that nothing we said would dissuade him. I also knew that if he was prepared to die we had to be prepared to die too. We might as well go right away and get it over with - hanging around (pardon the pun) would only prolong the agony. Oh yes, once I made up my mind I stuck by my decisions. I never decided until I believed the decision to be right.

After that horrible dark Friday when they crucified my master I was really afraid - we all were. I went off on my own to sort things out in my mind. And I suppose I thought that perhaps if I wasn't with the others who had gone around with Jesus the authorities might not come after me. So I kept off the streets and kept the doors locked, terrified that the next knock on the door would lead to the knock of hammer on nails for me. It seems that the others felt much the same but at least they were together when that first amazing appearance happened. When they told me the story it had all the makings of a dream. Just too fantastic for anyone, never mind me, to believe. Could you blame me for doubting? What would you think if someone told you that a friend who died a week ago had come back to life?

You'll have heard the story - how the stone had been rolled away from the entrance to the tomb. How the disciples were confused and fearful when they saw that the tomb was empty. And how Mary told them about seeing Jesus and how no one believed her. She was really upset but through tears and trauma she stuck to her story. Sometimes I wonder if she had moments of doubt herself. It's so easy to be influenced by other people, especially if they are your friends.

Anyway, that night suddenly Jesus was there with them. There in the room - despite the locked doors. At first they thought it was a ghost. Some of them said they found it difficult to believe their eyes. It was too good to be true. Jesus didn't do dazzling tricks to try to convince them - that was never his style - he just stayed there with them for a while. And soon they were convinced. Jesus was really there with them in that room. No ghost, but the living Christ. No longer wrapped in burial clothes and smelling of death but there in the flesh.

But I wasn't there and I could not believe them. People can come to believe all sorts of things if they really want to and I thought this was just wishful thinking. Just fantasising to help them through a bad time. I didn't really want to know.

Although I didn't believe the story, I missed my friends very much. After all, we had spent so much time together over the past three years. So I began to meet them again. We all respected and loved Jesus and what he stood for and I think part of me wanted to believe what they believed. But I needed evidence. I needed to see the marks of the nails. Only then could I be sure that Jesus was truly alive. For a whole week I struggled. The others were on a high and it would have been easy to get carried away, swept along with them. But that would have been against my nature.

Jesus knew me as well as I know myself - or better! He knew that nothing less than seeing him would persuade me. He wanted me to be sure so that I would remain a disciple. So he gave me what I wanted, what I needed, what I asked for - a personal experience. It was about a week after the others had seen Jesus that I saw him too. He didn't need a door to come into the room beside us but he certainly opened the door to belief for me.

"Peace be with you," he said. How I longed for that - the peace of not being in two minds, torn between belief and doubt. Then his eyes met mine. The hands he stretched out were torn and bruised from the tearing of the nails. Gently, one wounded hand took mine and placed it on his side. I could not bear to look but I could feel the long gash from the spear thrust. The cruelty of what had been done to my Lord was unbearable, yet in his eyes there was no hate or hurt, only love. The kind of love that is prepared to die for others. The kind of love that accepts people for what they are, with all their failings. The kind of love that knows what people need to help them through the toughest times. And believe me, having doubts about anything is a tough place to be. This I know to be true just as I now know the living Christ to be true.

'Doubting Thomas' they still call me. I think that's defamation of character! I do believe that Jesus rose from the dead and is with each one of us now. I trust what I saw and I trust the things he said. I'm very lucky; I saw Jesus. I realise I should not have needed that final experience to convince me. After all, I had been with him for three years, hearing all the things he said - including how he would die and yet would still be with us. I had heard but not understood. I still don't fully understand the mystery of that resurrection. But my experience convinces me that I don't need to understand fully in order to believe.

end

Reflection

There are many different words used in the New Testament translated only by one word in English – 'doubt'. While hesitating to get too far into the use of language in translation it is interesting to look some of the different ideas contained within our use of the word. It can describe someone who is chronically double-minded - *dipsukos* - as in the letter of James: 'a wave blown about by the wind' (James 1:6). If doubt can be defined as being in two minds about something, then to believe might be defined as being in one mind about it. To disbelieve could also be defined this way, so to doubt might be to waver between the two. Every culture seems to have a way of describing this irresolution. I like the Chinese one of 'having a foot in two boats' which is much more humorous than the English 'foot in two camps' and much less comfortable!

Here are some different words used to express doubt in the original Greek text:

diakrino: an inner state of mind so torn by various opinions that it can never come to a decision. Jesus says that mountains can be moved by those who have faith (Mark 11:23).

meteorizomai: 'to raise' or to 'suspend' - used figuratively to mean raising someone's hopes or to soar. Being lifted up in the air might be unsettling, leading to anxiety, tension and doubt - 'hung up' or 'up in the air' about something. Jesus used this word when he told the disciples not to be anxious about what they would eat or drink - the only time it's used in the New Testament (Luke 12:29).

dialogizomai: the root of our word 'dialogue' and describing an inner debate, reasoning things through in the mind. Usually this is used in the New Testament for the kind of reasoning which is wrong or evil. Jesus uses it when confronting the disciples after the Resurrection when they doubted the story told them by the two travellers who had met with him on the Emmaus road (Luke 24:38).

distazo: hesitating, faltering or hanging back, having reservations about something - Matthew uses this word when relates Jesus' words to Peter, who began to sink after stepping out of the boat so bravely (Matthew 14:31), and of those who doubted the risen Jesus (Matthew 28:17).

Why is it important to look at all these meanings? Because one word carries so many different ideas and this shows that doubt is not the opposite of faith, nor the same as unbelief. Faith is open to all possibilities and steps forwards bravely. Doubt is open to all possibilities but holds back and is reluctant to commit to something. Unbelief is being in one mind, being convinced that something is not to be believed. In Christian terms, unbelief is a state of mind closed to God, closed to the working of grace through Christ. Doubt can be expressed quite rightly by folk who find something difficult to accept but are open to being convinced: open to the working of Grace through Christ.

To express doubt can be a difficult and courageous thing to do. Admitting your feelings to others may leave you feeling silly – everyone else probably has no problem, or do they? Or perhaps you feel disloyal in some way – after all, everyone else in the church accepts that particular doctrine, don't they?

There will be someone, somewhere who shares my particular doubts. I'm not unique. By sharing we learn from each other – hearing of someone else's experience may tip the balance from doubt to faith. By acknowledging and giving voice to doubt, I open myself to God's grace and allow whatever I need to convince me to come into my life. If Thomas had pretended to believe, ignoring his doubts, he would never have received the invitation to touch the wounded hands and side. He would never have known the joy of being 'in one mind' about the truth of the Resurrection. Thinking back to the Chinese saying, would it have been long before the storms of life might have driven the two boats apart and Thomas's feet slipped between them into the sea of unbelief?

Have a candle placed ready to light later along with small pieces of paper, pens and a basket if you want to use the optional activity below. You will also need copies of Common Ground or a recording for the music item.

Question time

Group

Place three pieces of flip-chart paper on solid surfaces around the room, one for each question. You may wish to write up a suitable heading for each. People can write their thoughts on these 'Silent Walls' using large pens, or on 'post-it' notes which are then stuck on the sheets. (The leader may need to read out the list when answering the questions, especially if using post-it notes. Try to do this without comment unless clarification is needed).

Individual

If you are working on your own, make 3 lists for yourself.

Exercise

Everyone has their own perceptions about what 'the church' believes, about its practices, or its behaviour. There will be different perceptions of Biblical 'truth' (accepted or otherwise), about ordination or about the way the church spends its money.

• What beliefs, practices or perceptions about the church do you think people who have a Christian commitment generally struggle with? Try not to get too personal and try to avoid a long discussion (even with yourself!) over the different beliefs that folk hold.

• Think of those who describe themselves as Christian although they may not come to church. Do you think their struggles will be different or the same? Put comments from this question on the second sheet and highlight those on the first that are common.

• Now think of those who are not of any faith but who would not necessarily describe themselves as agnostic. Would they share the difficulties you have listed or are they likely to be different? Put these comments on the third sheet and highlight those on the first and second sheets that are common.

Look at the highlighted comments. Are there any that you as an individual or group could begin to address? It's most likely that there will be issues regarding how the church is seen to behave. Don't spend time trying to find solutions at this stage (or even worry that there are solutions!) – that would take too long. Note what you have found and think about how you could take it forward. This could be the basis for a discussion group at another time where a possible course of action could be decided upon. Don't just forget about it though – this is about being 'church' and breaking down walls we've built up over the centuries.

Now look at the first sheet. Pick out those (it may be all of them!) that are really about what we believe as Christians. How much do you (as a group) relate to that list? What do you struggle with? At this stage just acknowledge these issues, things which perhaps cause you to doubt. Don't get into a long theological discussion about any of them - that would be the next stage in a series of 'What I believe and Why' study sessions. You may want to decide now how you would like to do this. It is important that this is seen as the start of a process and is not allowed to drop.

Conclusion

Light the candle.
Take a few moments in silence to think about the whole idea of doubt and how you feel about what you have just heard or read.
(Optional activity) Take a piece of paper and draw a symbol representing something you have doubts about in your life of faith. You need not share what your symbol represents (unless you wish to) so be honest.
Sing or play a recording of 'When our confidence is shaken in beliefs we thought secure' (Common Ground 145) or a suitable alternative such as 'Look forward in faith' (Common Ground 73).
During the music the pieces of paper with the symbols of people's doubts can be placed into the basket. Don't throw away the symbols – they do matter. Think of a meaningful way of using them on some future occasion.

Prayer

God of creation,
You created your people with
ears to hear, eyes to see and minds to think.
We hear your voice, we see your wonderful world,
And sometimes we do not know what to think.
Sometimes even the molehills seem too big to move
And we turn a blind eye to the mountains.
Sometimes confidence is lost
And in hesitation we begin to sink.
Sometimes we are tossed in the storm of doubt
Our minds divided by questions with no answers.
Sometimes our hang-ups mean we are unnecessarily anxious,
unable to keep our feet on the ground of truth.
At these times we need to know you are with us.
We need to remember the times
When your wounded hand held ours
When your presence was real
When we knew your love for us was unfailing.
We need these times
In your Grace, we ask that you answer our need.
In our doubts and fears be with us Lord.

Amen